TIME MANAGEMENT FOR WRITERS

WRITE THIS WAY BOOK 1

AMANDA APTHORPE

ABOUT THE SERIES

Each volume in this *Write This Way* series is designed to address the needs, interests and concerns that have emerged from my years of teaching creative writing to students in undergraduate degrees and short courses, from my academic engagement with the national and international writing communities, and from my own writing practice.

While many students/class participants and solo writers have great intentions of completing a writing project, few will see it through, claiming that there is too little time. As such, this guide on **time management** is the first in the series to establish patterns or rituals of writing that will sustain the journey to completion.

Once established, writers can hone their craft by following subsequent editions that include – finding your writing voice; characterization and point of view; plot and structure; dialogue, description and setting; and the editing toolbox.

Each volume takes the writer step-by-step through specific elements of writing, providing useful strategies, opportunities for reflection, for learning current research, and to write. The inclusion of space within each volume for the writing exercises and reflections provides a record that can be reflected upon at a later time.

INTRODUCTION

Dear Reader

May I ask: Are you a procrastinator? Is that why you've picked up/downloaded this book?

If so, you have company. Procrastinating about undertaking tasks, especially if it's been imposed or is not desirable, is a common problem. That seems quite reasonable. However, procrastinating even when the task is something you really want to do, like writing a novel, short story, research paper, poem ... that's a bigger problem.

OR

Perhaps you're not a procrastinator, but you just don't have enough time to do what you need to do or what you want to do. There are so many other demands: raising a family, enjoying and maintaining friendships and a social life; work and/or study; other hobbies; travel ... and the list goes on. These are legitimate time stealers, and most, if not all, are very pleasant. You feel guilty if you write and think that perhaps it's just a little bit (or very) self-indulgent.

OR

You have all the time in the world but find yourself staring at a blank page or screen and time feels like a weight on your shoulders. What's even worse is that you feel guilty that you're not writing. You think of all those hours that you could have written and ...

In any case, you're making a good choice if you read on. Achieving your writing goals and fulfilling your writing dream are within your hands.

In the pages that follow, you will:

- Identify your motivation for writing

- Understand the relationship between motivation and goal setting
- Learn why goal setting can assist you in fulfilling your writing dream
- Establish your own long- and short-term goals
- Marvel at the magic of 10 minutes
- Recognise your writing threshold and work with it
- Build neural pathways
- Write and write some more
- Learn how to become opportunistic
- Find time to do other pleasurable activities
- Still love your family and friends
- Still be loved by your family and friends

You will achieve these through:

- Reflective writing
- Spontaneous writing
- Stating clear long- and short-term goals
- Counting words
- Hearing what the experts have to say
- Useful tips and strategies

This book is geared towards the writer completing a larger work – a novel but can be applied across all creative writing styles. It is designed for you to work through a process that asks you to reflect and respond, write, establish goals and practise them. You might decide to read straight through, but the best effects will be gained by travelling step-by-step. It's up to you.

What you'll find in this book are questions that ask for a response (space is given for writing should you prefer to keep it all together); writing exercises; research findings; tips; quotes of inspiration; and a journal template. I have also included personal anecdotes about my own experience and thoughts.

So ... let's get you on your way.

MOTIVATION

SO, you want to write?

I did. It wasn't a burning passion that kept me awake at nights dreaming of being an impoverished writer in a Parisian attic, but rather, it was something that snuck up on me.

I dithered and doodled and managed to write a few short stories that, reading back on them now, were 'cute'. I didn't have a big dream - that came later, but I did decide I wanted to learn more about this writing thing.

You see, I didn't study literature or finish my Year 12 English, for that matter. I didn't get to read hefty tomes that might have inspired me and shown me the way. Oh, I read, but by seventeen, I was married and a mother, my education was curtailed, and I didn't go to university until I was twenty-six. By then, I'd met my current partner, and between us, we had three children. So, I took myself back to school and trained to be a science teacher. But that's another story.

Those 'cute' little stories written in spare moments began to accumulate, and my desire to learn grew. The following is the trajectory of my writing life to date, most of it tucked into the sides of the full-time life as a science teacher, partner, mother and later, grandmother:

- Correspondence course (I think they went out of business before I finished it)
- Short creative writing course at the CAE (Centre for Adult Education where I now teach). This felt like such a luxury at the time. I'd taken my first batch of long service leave and thought I'd entertain the idea of being a writer. It was in this class that I received the first feedback that suggested I wasn't too bad at all at writing. That was enough to make me want more.

- Professional Writing and Editing at RMIT (I enrolled as a part-time student to undertake a class of creative writing after work one night a week. When I went in to enrol, I had no idea what unit I wanted to do. Short story (because of those cute ones) was the obvious choice, or poetry. I was at the back of the line, and by the time I got to the counter, the only thing left was 'Novel Writing'. 'Okay,' I said. And so it began. My first novel began here).

- Master of Arts at Melbourne University (my first novel was completed here)
- PhD (Creative Arts) Melbourne University (my second novel and an exegesis on mythic structures in Australian women's literature were completed here).

You'll have your own story, the reasons you came to writing. Remind yourself here:

....

....

....

You could argue that I didn't really need to do all these courses. And you'd be right! However, what I've determined over these ten years of teaching creative writing in undergraduate degrees, TAFE, and short courses is that some of us want/need/like to rise to the expectation of someone else. For myself, it had a lot to do with a lack of confidence in assessing my own worth. I didn't want to fool myself that I was good when perhaps I wasn't. I had a family and a mortgage and, quite frankly, I didn't want to waste anyone's time.

I have taught hundreds of people who dream of writing a novel (or other). Their intention is sincere, their dream is strong, but the harsh reality is that most of them will abandon the dream. The problem lies partly in the fact that it remains a dream rather than becoming a goal.

The ideas, strategies and theories presented here have been developed in response to this reality. I want my students and you, who are also my writing peers, to achieve their/your writing dreams.

So, let's begin by looking at yours. You'll need a pen and this book, or a computer.

What's your motivation?

Record your responses to the following questions in the space that follows, or type and save. It's good to have a record to revisit later. Give yourself a few minutes to think and to write for each. Take your time. It's always a pleasure to write anyway, isn't it?

What do you like to write (write about)? (e.g., mother's biography, political intrigue, a contemporary coming-of-age story)

....

....

....

....

Of course, everyone is going to have their personal preferences, but this is significant. Identifying your preferences, your likes/dislikes is important to finding your own voice. You won't be motivated if you're copying someone else. It has to be about you.

Why do you like to write? What do you get out of it?

....

....

....

....

Frequent responses include: the sense of flow or immersion - time 'stands still'; the satisfaction of doing something for yourself; sorting things out in your mind or about the world; creating new worlds and different experiences; the pleasure of words; to win the Booker Prize.

What are your dreams (desires/hopes) for your writing?

....

....

....

Frequent responses include: to finish the book; for the satisfaction of knowing I've done it; to write my mother's story; to satisfy a long-held need; to be published.

Take a break. Take a breath.

Is there anything that concerns you about writing? (Examples of this might include - I'm not good enough; I'm not going to finish it; I don't have the time; I'm not going to be published.)

....

....

....

....

The typical responses are those above. I'll share one of mine that's not included there: I sometimes fear the immersion itself. Why? Because I have many other aspects of my life waiting in the wings, and they can be very demanding. Immersing myself can mean I don't want to come out of it when there's a meal that needs to be cooked or other. Perhaps you can relate.

Pause. Now, this is the big one:

How much do you really want to do this? How important is it to you? Be very honest with yourself.

....

....

....

....

There isn't a typical response to this. However, it's very important that *you* know the answer. If you're half-hearted, I suggest you don't keep going (though, of course, you might be stimulated by the end of the book and be full-hearted!).

To write to the end is to be brave. Consider this: What's at stake if you don't do it?

Think about that and write it here:

If I don't do this

....

....

....

I believe that it is important to you to finish your writing project; otherwise, you wouldn't have acquired this guide.

You're undertaking a journey that will have its measure of ups and downs as any interesting journey has. Yes, you do need to be brave, but you don't actually have to do this, do you? You want to do it, isn't that correct? So rather than gritting your teeth and steeling yourself for the road ahead, what if we travel it together with a light-hearted sense that it will be one of the best trips you've ever taken.

Determining your motivation to undertake a writing project is essential for goal setting, the next step in our process, and there is a reciprocal relationship between them. That is, the more motivated you are, the more likely you are to achieve your goals, and, as you set goals and achieve them, your motivation is increased.

Motivation can be intrinsically generated, for example, the desire to create

QUITE INTERESTING

The findings of Teresa Amabile's study (1985) showed that writers who were extrinsically motivated to write (i.e. motivated to engage in a writing task by external goals such as the promise of reward or the expectation of evaluation) were temporarily less creative than those who were intrinsically motivated to engage in a particular task (i.e. motivated primarily by their own interest or involvement) (393).

Although Amabile's research indicated that writers were more creative when intrinsically motivated, in those moments when the writing starts to feel like work, extrinsic motivation (e.g. teacher direction and expectation) may be the best motivation available (Baer and McKool).

According to Robert Sternberg, intrinsic motivation is not something inherent in a person, instead one decides to be motivated and to look for ways to make a task more interesting (88).

beautiful prose. Alternatively, extrinsic motivation relies on an external factor, such as the prospect of being published. A grey area might be when you want to improve your writing skills (intrinsic) and put in more effort if it is to be assessed by a teacher or workshopped with peers (extrinsic). This is one of the reasons why writing courses are so popular, though once the extrinsic motivator (teacher/peers) is removed, the intrinsic motivation can wane. See Teresa Amabile's study

Amabile identified seven reasons for writing being defined as intrinsic: getting pleasure out of reading something you have written; enjoying the opportunity for self-expression; achieving new insights through your writing; deriving satisfaction from expressing yourself clearly and eloquently; feeling relaxed when writing; enjoying the play with words; enjoying becoming involved with ideas, characters, events and images in your writing (396).

This book works from the premise that time management techniques can lead to greater creativity, and that intrinsic motivation can be enhanced by building a daily pattern to help sustain the writing journey. This is not to suggest that extrinsic motivation is the bad guy. It's what got me off the verandah (I'll explain more later.) to take the first step as an almost unemployable mother of three, to fulfil a dream of having her own home. See what Baer and McKool say

What's important here is to determine the level of your motivation. Whether intrinsic, extrinsic or a blend, the deeper your desire to complete something, the more likely you will. There's good news, too, for those who feel like they haven't been blessed with a motivational wand at birth. See Sternberg

That sounds easy, doesn't it? If that's the case, and you have already determined from your responses earlier that your motivation is strong, then perhaps it's unnecessary to read on.

But wait. We need to have a talk - about the elephant in the room. The big P (or R) - Procrastination (or Resistance).

Before we go there, let's take a writing break. (Hang on! That's just procrastinating talking about procrastination! Well spotted. We'll tackle it in the next chapter).

EXERCISE 1: SPONTANEOUS WRITING

GO with it and trust me on this one. There is a point.

I'm going to give you a lead-in of a few words for you to continue in any way you like. If you're in the process of writing something (novel, short story ...), perhaps steer it to that. It's up to you.

However, as much as is possible, switch off your internal editor and just write for 10 minutes.

Don't take your pen off the page or your fingers off the keys. If you don't know what to write, then write that! *'I don't know what to write, but Amanda says I have to and ...'*

Set your timer for 10 minutes. You can use the space below if you would like to. Here are your words:

There are times when

....

....

....

....

....

....

....

....

....

....

....

....

....

....

....

....

....

....

....

Now that you're back:

As you can see, I've called this exercise 'spontaneous writing', otherwise known as 'free-flow' or 'stream of consciousness', and we'll do more of this as we travel together. Add up the number of words you wrote in that 10-minute exercise and record it somewhere.

PROCRASTINATION

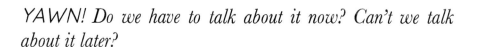

Time Quotes

If you don't write when you don't
have time for it, you won't write
when you do have time for it

Katerina Stoykova Klemer

YAWN! Do we have to talk about it now? Can't we talk about it later?

The simple definition of procrastination, sometimes known as the 'pleasure principle', is the action of delaying or postponing something, typically because it is unpleasant or boring.

What is of concern is that procrastination is also the action of delaying or postponing something we like, even love, something we might want very, very much - such as writing a novel, or our mother's biography of her travels up the Nile, or our father's muffin cookbook.

One of the reasons that procrastination is a common problem is because it's an excellent strategy for avoiding failure. After all, it has an evolutionary advantage allowing us to stop and consider our options (or our surroundings) before launching in and making poor choices (or being eaten).

In my years of teaching creative writing, the most common excuse given for not completing a writing task is 'life just got so hectic this week' or words to that effect. Of course, life does have its moments of becoming incredibly busy, often unexpectedly, and writing might indeed need to be put on the back burner to accommodate it. However, it's when this becomes the pattern of excuse that is the problem.

Fear of failing can be crippling, particularly when, as creative writers, we're exposing our thoughts, imagination and skills to others, or perhaps even to just ourselves. Fear of failure can be a reflection of low self-confidence or perfectionist anxiety that might be disguising low self-confidence.

Workshopping is a typical component of a creative writing class and for good reason. As writers working in isolation, it can be very difficult to objectively determine the quality of our own work. We can think it's fabulous, when perhaps it's not and, more often, we can think it's dreadful, when in fact it's not. Workshopping, when managed by a competent teacher who establishes the reasons for the process (e.g. providing constructive feedback to the writer on what works and what might work better), is often the favourite part of a writing class. That's what I tell my students in the first week, and I try to reassure them that, despite their anxiety, they will get a lot out of it.

I see their trepidation when we discuss how the next week's first workshop will unfold. If the class is an optional short course, I remind them in an email beforehand that it's worth continuing the course and to not be put off by the idea of sharing their work. It's understandable to be nervous, I tell them and then hold my breath as I take the attendance roll the following week. Of all the hundreds of students I have taught, only two have not come back. For the others, yes, they're nervous in that first workshop; some might even take up the option of a walk while the others (usually small groups) read their work, but by the end of that first night, it's a whole different story. Not only have they connected with their writing peers and realised that all the others were as nervous as they were, but I see their pride and their hunger to learn. Everyone comes back the next week and the next ... and some continue well after the course is finished to meet and share their work.

To write is to be brave. If you have no intention of letting anyone else read it – ever – but simply want to see if you can complete a writing project, then perhaps there's no need for others to provide you with feedback. However, most of us, including me, have that old extrinsic motivation – to be published spurring us on. If you hold the manuscript close to your chest until it's sitting on an editor's desk, it's a bit late. While I have listed wanting to be published under the extrinsic motivation heading, it's a worthy motivator because there's nothing like having a reader – someone you connect with through your words, and it's better to know that you're making that sort of connection, or not, as you go.

This is a favourite picture on the wall of my study:

That's what most of us want as readers and as writers, isn't it?

Self-esteem + Self-efficacy --------> Self-confidence

Self-esteem: general feelings of self-worth and self-value

Self-efficacy: belief in one's capacity to succeed at tasks

Note that in the equation above, the level of confidence we have in ourselves (e.g. to finish a specific task and to finish it well) is a result of our general feelings of self-worth and self-value (self-esteem), plus the belief in our own general capacity to succeed at tasks (self-efficacy).

You'll have an idea about your own level of self-esteem – it's been built up or shot down by your personal circumstances. Tackling it here is beyond the scope of this book. However, that doesn't mean that if your self-esteem is as low as that, you can stop reading. As a result of success using the strategies in this book, you might well find that your self-worth and self-value are given a boost. And they can always do with a boost.

We can talk more openly about your self-efficacy, and we'll begin with another series of questions to reflect on it.

Ready? Let's go:

Have there been times when you **haven't** followed something through; you haven't completed the job, the course, the painting of the house, the jigsaw puzzle … If yes, record them here:

....

....

....

....

Why? Can you identify any triggers that stopped you?

....

....

....

....

Could you have completed it/them if you'd wanted to?

....

....

How do you feel about yourself when you **don't** finish a task, especially if it's one you wanted to finish?

....

....

What have you seen through to the end? (It/They don't have to be anything to do with writing). If relevant record here:

....

....

....

....

What type of motivation enabled you to see it/them through – intrinsic (from within you), or extrinsic (from without you), or both?

....

....

What strategies did you use to complete it/them? (e.g. turned off the television; didn't go out; pushed on during the rough patches; talked about it with someone else ...)

....

....

....

How do you feel about yourself when you **do** finish a task?

....

....

Let's focus on the tasks you did finish. Could you apply any of the strategies above to your writing life? Record them here:

....

....

....

If you are not very good at seeing things through to the end, don't go away! I'm here to work with you on that.

Whether you have finished tasks or never finished tasks, complete the following:

My capacity to complete tasks is

....

....

....

The triggers that can prevent me from finishing a task are

....

....

The strategies I could employ or have employed to finish a task could be/are

....

....

....

Now that you have an idea of what your own self-efficacy looks like, and perhaps it's not great, let's start to build it up. The wonderful thing about having or building a belief in your ability to finish a task (self-efficacy) is that it can help to increase your self-esteem.

Previously, when I listed the courses I've undertaken on my writing journey, I mentioned that the need for feedback came out of a lack of confidence in my own ability. I needed someone to tell me I was good or not. Prior to that writing journey, I had completed a Bachelor of Education that enabled me to become a science teacher. That was done full-time, with a toddler in tow and two at school, and a weekend job serving breakfasts to motel rooms, so I had already started to get the idea that I could finish things. The thing is, I didn't know that before. My history didn't demonstrate it. I hadn't finished high school, nor the secretarial course that followed. On becoming pregnant at sixteen, I was told that my life was over (good grief!). So, I had little self-esteem, which continued for quite a while, but I started to build a picture of myself as having good self-efficacy. I could finish stuff, and that started to make me feel good about myself.

The point of that story is that to build self-confidence in your ability to complete your writing project, you can start with building self-efficacy. Of course, some of you might have excellent self-efficacy, but for some reason, you just can't seem to sustain this writing journey. You need to read on too.

GOAL SETTING

There is abundant research evidence to suggest that, in order to overcome procrastination, we should set goals.

Read what Sonja Lyubomirsky says

I suggest that whether you procrastinate or not, whether you have little time to write, or too much (but that's still procrastination), goal setting is an important strategy towards fulfilling your writing dreams.

QUITE INTERESTING

An increase in wellbeing is most likely when a person chooses and attains self-concordant goals, that is, goals that 'fit' the person (Lyubomirsky et al 2005).

Edwin A Locke confirms that goals that are most effective need to be specific, challenging yet attainable and are more likely to be attained when made public and believes that we should write them down (2008).

Taj Ben-Shahar says in his book *Happier* (2007) that, among other things, the goals we set need to be self-concordant.

Sigh … another 'selfie', but this one is warm and friendly, and the definition goes like this:

Self-concordant goals are goals that are aligned with who we are, our authentic self and with what we want to do in our lives' (Faucheux 2012).

Had this book been targeted to anyone who needs to manage time, then this 'selfie' might require more reflection and navel-gazing. However, for you as a creative writer, I'm doubting that anyone is co-ercing you into writing, even yourself. I'm assuming that you *want* to write and that you *want* to finish your writing project (and then start the next one, of course). And that somewhere along the line, you identified this as self-concordant, a recognition that the niggling urge for self-expression needed an outlet.

This is great news! It saves you a considerable amount of sorting yourself out and means that establishing goals should be quite straightforward. And it is.

Where you might run into problems is sticking to those goals because there are all sorts of minefields out there to interrupt your best-laid plans. You're going to learn ways of identifying and negotiating your way around those minefields.

As well as advising that goals be self-concordant, Ben-Shahar and others recommend that they be specific, so in the question that follows, I'm asking you to do just that. Be specific and try to keep it as simple as possible. Why?

Let's see what Locke has to say:

YOUR LONG TERM GOAL

What is the long-term goal for your writing? (e.g. to complete the novel; to be published …)

That should be the easy part, but the problem can be that the idea of what we want is 'fluffy' or 'vague', and our brain can't visualise a fluffy, vague idea. If it's the engine that will enable you to fulfil your dream, then you have to do better than that. Really, it's your servant. Tell the brain what you want, visualise it so that it can see some detail, and then it will do its best to bring it about. Fluffy concept, fluffy process.

Here's a long-term goal I'll admit to with some embarrassment. While writing my very first novel, my long-term goal was to win the Nobel Prize for Literature (you've got to give me some credit for being specific and dreaming big!).

How big is this project? Can you give an approximate size? (e.g. a novel is $80,000 - 120,000$ words).

. . . .

When do you want to have this project completed (to final edit)? Why then?

. . . .

How achievable is it to complete the project by then? Will you need to undertake some skills training? Will there be non-writing times that you know of?

Do you need to reconsider the timeframe? Be realistic, a large project like a novel can take years.

If you are sure of your target, write it here in month and year.

. . . .

What will be the reward for completing this project? (e.g. self-satisfaction, a bottle of expensive champagne, a trip away, a party, a good sleep). If you hadn't thought of one, try it now. Research tells us that the prospect of reward – long term and short term – helps us overcome procrastination.

....

You might even feel that you don't need an extrinsic reward, that going forward is a reward in itself. If so, well done.

Perhaps you're thinking at this point that this process is far too pedantic, the antithesis of what you think creative writing should be.

Sankalpa

Recognising that we are perfectly imperfect, a Sankalpa is an intention formed by the heart or mind; a one-pointed resolve to focus on a specific goal.

Well … perhaps, but time is not creative, it's just seconds, minutes and hours (okay, it's a man-made construct, and that's rather creative), and the number of words you need to call your project a novel or short story …is simply arithmetic. How you put together your words in time is the creative part, but you are a wordsmith. This is the craft, hobby, experiment you have chosen. You have given yourself a task, a pleasurable one, I hope, one that you want, and you need to deliver the words.

A personal anecdote and back to getting off the step of the verandah:

I mentioned above that it had been extrinsic motivation that propelled me to make a big decision as an unskilled mother of three – to have our own home. I was sitting on the verandah of our rental and daydreaming as is my want, and knew that if life was to change, I had to act on my dreams – I had to have a goal. I got up, went inside to call a local high school (no mobiles then!) and enrolled myself in a night course to undertake Biology and Mathematics at Year 12 level (I hadn't done Year 12, and my last math's class was way back in Year 10). That decision resulted in me becoming a teacher, and a similar one made by my partner changed the course of our lives. It was a powerful motivator, so I'm all for the extrinsic.

However, while I loved and still love being a teacher, there was this other dream – to be a writer that was niggling away in the background. Hence the courses that I listed above were my practical way of bringing it into reality. This was a very intrinsic goal – a self-concordant goal that became so strong that I began to dream of making even bigger steps towards the life of a writer. As happens in life, once ready to act, certain things happen. I was asked to be a guinea pig for a girl studying to become a life coach. Reluctantly at first, I agreed. During a phone call, she asked me to think of a time when I had made a big decision before. Where was I? How did I feel? Well, of course, I knew that was the verandah of the rental house many years before. I thought of how significantly the odds were against me fulfilling the dream at that stage, but how I acted on it, with a simple phone call. And I began to cry. If I could do it then, I thought, I can do it now. When my first novel was published, I decided to take a leap of faith and, like the original one, it required me to act. I left my job after twenty-five years and began to make space for writing. In my case, at least, it came down to having a dream, shaping it into a goal, then taking it on in bite-sized steps.

Here are some favourite quotes you might have read before that can help sustain the journey and feed our confidence:

Whatever you can do, or dream you can, begin it! Boldness has genius, magic, and power in it. Goethe

I say, follow your bliss and don't be afraid, and doors will open where you didn't know they were going to be. Joseph Campbell

That said, let's get to the nitty-gritty – setting smaller goals.

Among the reasons discussed so far that can waylay us in our writing journey (procrastination, no time) is the daunting prospect of writing, if a novel, up to 120,000 words (or more).

As for many tasks in life, if we focus too much on the target, the size of the task, we can become overwhelmed and paralysed. Making lists is a common way of breaking tasks up, and there's something very satisfying about physically crossing each hurdle off.

100,000 words is the size of a PhD thesis! At least for that, you get something to hang on the wall and a title. So why would anyone in their right mind want to tackle something that big when there's a possibility that it won't be published no matter how good it is?

Well, you wrote the answer to that one at the beginning. 'Why do you like to write?' 'What do you get out of it?' Every now and then, revisit your response. I don't know what you've written, but I'll offer this well-rubbed gem.

It's not about the goal … it's about the journey. Ben-Shahar emphasises that the importance of goal setting lies within the journey it takes to reach the destination, and Watson thinks so too.

We need to think of goals as a means and not an end.

Clichéd though the idea might sound, it's true.

Remember my Nobel Prize dream? I recall that I was sitting up in bed one morning and looking out the window, allowing my imagination to run wild. I dared to dream that my first novel was so good I was awarded the prize. I saw myself walking up the stairs to the stage and receiving the medal (and the cheque). And then a strange thing happened. Up there, on the stage of my imagination, I felt suddenly deflated. The journey that had sustained me for several years was over. I loved my characters, I loved the process of learning, and I think I loved my innocence and wonder at being a first-time writer.

I believe this experience is common amongst those who have had success achieving their goals, whether it be in writing, business, music, or any other venture where they dared to dream. It certainly happens to writers because what do they do when they've finished that PhD sized manuscript without the guarantee of success? They do it again, and again, and again.

I felt calm after that experience. I knew then that it truly is the journey that's the best part of all.

So … get your backpack ready, and I'll start loading in the supplies to sustain you on the road. The following quotes are the first to go in:

A person is a fool to become a writer. His only compensation is absolute freedom. He has no master except his own soul, and that, I am sure, is why he does it. Roald Dahl, *Boy*.

If I cannot be myself in what I write, then the whole thing is nothing but lies and humbug. Henrik Ibsen

YOUR SHORT-TERM GOALS

There's something very satisfying about lists – mental or hard copy – the ticking or striking off as you go. They're a very popular tool for managing the tasks we need to do by thinking or writing them down.

The items in a list are written or thought in succinct, specific language. This in itself reduces the perceived size of a task or the number of them to perform. The whole 'to do' list is seen as being composed of do-able/achievable bites, and the overall task becomes shorter – the target of completion in sight.

You know the size of your writing project; you've estimated the number of words and, perhaps, a timeframe in which to complete it. A realistic timeframe, of course.

Let's take some steps on our journey to break it up into do-able/achievable bites that are satisfying in themselves, perhaps even inspiring, but enable you to see that the destination is not as far away - or as daunting - as you thought:

STEP 1: MAKE A DATE
STEP 2: THE MAGIC OF 10 MINUTES
STEP 3: DO THE ARITHMETIC
STEP 4: RESET THE TARGET

STEP 1

MAKE A DATE

CONSIDER the timetable below this page. What are the times you know are non-negotiable for writing in your average week (work, meetings, meals, family time, hobby commitments, sleep)? No need to fill them in. You probably have a very clear idea of this anyway.

Locate 10 minutes on each of the 7 days when you would be able to write. Try to make it approximately the same time each day, but if that's not possible, just ensure that you have 10 minutes every day. Don't leap ahead and think – *I don't have 10 minutes!* Yes, you do. You just might need to free up time by organising the other things differently. I'll wager that if you were suddenly asked to do something extra (write up the minutes to a meeting, babysit, have lunch with a friend who's just dropped into town, read another chapter of that riveting novel), you'd find that time.

Is the time you have chosen when you feel creative or when you might be exhausted? Ideally, try to choose a creative time. If you're a lark, is there time in the morning? Can you get up 10-15 minutes earlier? If you're an owl, can you stay up 10-15 minutes later?

You might resist this process because you prefer to write in longer chunks of time. Perhaps you're adept at writing for three hours every now and then. I'm not suggesting you lose your own methods. Far from it. However, if you're reading this book, there's a strong chance that your method is not getting you across the line, so go with me on this one, at least for a while.

Now enter it into the timetable and consider it to be non-negotiable – it's only 10 minutes, but I need to say here that, should you find you get on a roll and you want to go longer, by all means – go longer! It's **a minimum of 10 minutes**.

Nearly all of my earlier writings (degrees and novels) were tucked in around full-time teaching. As I'm a lark and my most creative time is early in the morning, I chose this time to write. This usually meant getting up somewhere before 6am, showering, eating breakfast and then down the street to the coffee shop opposite the railway station. Over a cup of coffee, I would write intensely for 10 minutes or more. I didn't establish the 10-minute rule; instead, it became a pattern because that was all I had available. But it was so effective that it's still my practice today. I can afford to take longer, and I do, but on those days when there are other demands, no less. If there are lots of things going on, I get up even earlier.

So, decide on your 10-minute time and make a date on the timetable that follows (or other).

NB – this is a time for writing, not researching or editing. We can justify that we're working on the project when we're doing these things; however, that has to be done at another time. This is about getting the words down. You've got a lot of them to write.

	Sun	Mon	Tues	Wed	Thurs	Fri	Sat
12am-1am							
1am-2am							
2am-3am							
3am-4am							
4am-5am							
5am-6am							
6am-7am							
7am-8am							
8am-9am							
9am-10am							
10am-11am							
11am-12pm							
12pm-1pm							
1pm-2pm							
2pm-3pm							
3pm-4pm							
4pm-5pm							
5pm-6pm							
6pm-7pm							
7pm-8pm							
8pm-9pm							
9pm-10pm							
10pm-11pm							

Exercise 2: Spontaneous Writing

Use the space below if there's enough room. Here are your lead-in words:

There was a fragrance

....

....

....

....

....

....

....

....

....

....

....

....

....

....

....

....

....

....

....

Count the number of words you've written in that 10 minutes and record them.

STEP 2

THE MAGIC OF 10 MINUTES

YOU'VE NOW MADE a 10 minute-per-day date with your writing. *What*, you may ask, *am I going to write in that time?*

That's up to you. You can write anything you want in the two weeks, but there is a condition: you must keep writing – your pen must keep flowing across the page or your fingers dancing across the keys, but ... does this sound familiar? These are the same rules for the Spontaneous Writing exercises.

You've done two of these exercises now. I gave you lead-in words, and you wrote (I hope) for the 10 minutes required. That's exactly what you're going to do – **every day for 2 weeks.** It's only 10 minutes after all.

If you're feeling a little bit lost, I've supplied some lead-ins here for each day of the first week that you can use if you want to. Here they are:

Day 1: The week began …
Day 2: There will always be …
Day 3: There was a sensation of …
Day 4: Behind the …
Day 5: The terms and conditions …
Day 6: Suddenly, the sky …
Day 7: 'Please, never …'

Of course, you don't need to use any of these. Make up your own. I did, as I was writing this. The magic doesn't lie within the lead-ins. They're just sentence fragments that you can make up; borrow from the newspaper next to you or the first words in a sentence from the book or magazine you're currently reading. Once you're on your way, begin steering them in the direction of the project.

In the first two weeks, you're going to have to spot check and be accountable, and one of the best ways to do this is to keep a diary or journal. You'll find a template (Appendix) you can use at the back of this book. When you are making your entries, be honest with yourself. Did you write each day? If not, what were the distractions? Did you use the 10 minutes you originally allocated, or did you find other times better? Did you stop because you didn't feel inspired? If you don't succeed in writing every day for one week, keep it up for another week.

QUITE INTERESTING ¶

In her article 'The Writers Brain: What Neurology Tells Us About Teaching Creative Writing' (2010), Rosanne Bane states that the potential conflict between the limbic system and the cerebral cortex accounts for writer's block and other forms of writer's resistance. When the limbic system is stimulated, behaviour is instinctual based on the fight-or-flight response. The effect is to limit the input from the cerebral cortex thus temporarily depriving the ability for creative thought (2). Bane suggests that instructors can help students overcome this conflict by promoting writing habits and routines. 'Writing rituals take advantage of Hebb's Law, which states that neurons that fire together, wire together' (6). ¶

¶

You might prefer your own process of writing intensely at weekends, but is it a ritual? Has this process served you well enough to keep you on track, or do things often happen at that time to disrupt it?

However, you might find during this exercise above that you begin to develop a different ritual to that suggested. If that's the case, keep it up until you feel that it has truly become ritualised.

AND THE POINT IS ...

The results of Zampetakis, Bouranta and Mous-takis' 2010 study on the relationship between time management and creativity indicated that individual creativity is positively related to daily planning behaviour (27).

What you're doing when you establish a ritual or routine is to establish a neurological connection between your brain and your writing habits. This means that new neurological pathways result in the brain understanding what it has to do in that writing time. The effect of this is to reduce the amount of time you spend pondering, procrastinating, or resisting writing down those words. You'll get better and sink deeper more quickly into flow (see later) because you've trained your mind to do so.

That is why the writing instruction for these 10 minutes, and for the Spontaneous Writing exercises, is to write anything and keep writing. It's not the quality of the work you're training for initially - it's to build habits. You're taking advantage of **Hebb's Law**. See Rosanne Bane in QI.

A daily writing practice, at the same time of day or night, assists the establishment of writing as an integral component of a writer's everyday life. Rituals create new neural pathways, soothe the limbic brains so that the cerebral cortex can function optimally (Bane 8).

I can vouch for this by drawing on my own experience. The minimum of 10 minutes in the coffee shop before work each morning is now so engrained in my psyche that I don't feel right if I don't do it. I liken it to not having a shower or that first cup of coffee. If, for some unexpected reason, I miss it, I feel a subtle inner turmoil. Once this integral component of my daily life is satisfied, I'm ready for the many other aspects of my day.

However, that said, I know that other things in life can sabotage the plan. When two of our grandchildren were just five and six years old, they were placed in our care, a situation that lasted for nearly eight years. At those ages, they were too young for me to continue that particular process at weekends unless I took them with me – and that didn't really work. I had to develop other strategies that I'll talk more about under 'Resilience'. As they got older, I was able to reestablish it.

 TIP: Put away technology or any other distractions, unplug the Web, turn off the television.

DON'T WAIT FOR INSPIRATION

Locating a minimum of 10 minutes to write and, ideally, the best time to write is effective in establishing time management skills and in merging the concept of the writing self with the daily self. However, most writers know that the blank page or screen can sometimes be daunting and demanding of our best. There can be a moment of freezing, the uncertainty of where to begin – the limbic system is in ascendance.

Spontaneous writing (stream of consciousness or free flow) is a common tool for teachers of creative writing because it's an effective means of engaging students immediately in the writing process. The random placement of the two exercises in this book provides an unexpected and perhaps unsettling start to a writing task, and the lead-in words might have little bearing on the immediate experience. In my writing classes, I begin this way. I don't wait for the students to settle – some of them are tired, others feeling rushed from work, or others are just not in the mood. This is the reality of writing. We're not always in creative mode, we don't always feel inspired, but we need to break through and keep going anyway.

By establishing the 10-minute ritual, by building neurological pathways, by borrowing or making up lead-in words and launching in, we often find that the writing produces its own momentum and immersion or flow can occur more quickly.

When you look at the whole view of the timetable in which you've included your daily 10 minutes, you'll notice that there's a lot of empty space – a whole page devoted to empty spaces! See it as a visual reminder that the rest of your life has *plenty* of time allocated to it, and what you're asking for here is so little in comparison.

Before we go any further, let's do another Spontaneous Writing exercise. (Why now, you ask? Aren't we in the middle of something? Yes. That's the point, and you'll learn why later).

The same conditions apply: 10 minutes to write, turn off your internal editor if possible, don't take your pen off the page or fingers off the keys. Put your phone away.

DO SET CHALLENGING AND INSPIRING GOALS

Consider these 10 minutes initially like a training ground. Set challenging and inspiring goals that you will look forward to. (If goals are seen as mundane or do not stimulate you by challenging your ability – not too much, just a bit, you're less likely to continue to the end.)

For example:

- Examine a section of writing by your favourite author and use a sentence fragment from it as your lead-in. Try writing like them. Don't worry, you're not going to end up writing like them; just use the exercise to think about how they might craft it.

- Step outside the genres you usually read and try something you normally avoid or have little interest in. Try writing during your 10 minutes in this style. There's something to learn in any writing style. You might be surprised.
- Play with words/ideas. Experiment with making up your own metaphors. Let yourself go.

VALUE YOUR WRITING

How much do you value your writing time? What evidence is there that you do?

Even if you have to steal a corner of the kitchen table, make it somewhere you want to be. For example, keep that favourite cup beside you; buy a new pen and notebook, or wipe over the screen and keyboard to signify that this is special time.

These days I have my own study, and I have surrounded myself with things that have meaning for me – things that represent in some way who I am (though mind you, I look at the collection of things at times and wonder if perhaps I'm a little bit odd!). I love that it's my space and that I devote it to all things writing (and yoga). However, this luxury of having my own room has taken its time to arrive. I've had desks in all sorts of areas of the house and have had to pack up and move when the grandchildren came, as my partner had to give over his studio. As I've mentioned, most of my writing took place in the coffee shop just up the road. I had to go outside my home to find somewhere to be. In those early days, I would have been comforted to know that a certain single mother was doing the same on the other side of the world and that Harry Potter came alive in a coffee shop!

It's wonderful to have your own space – desk in the corner of the bedroom, whole study all to yourself. All good things. But don't become dependent on them. Train yourself to write in most circumstances; that way, you can use those random free moments you weren't expecting.

One of the most moving stories of finding your space is that told by Stephen King. Following the horrific accident when he was hit by a car while on his daily constitutional walk, he was hospitalized for a long period. When he returned to his home, in a wheelchair, he could no longer work at his desk nor wanted to write at all. On the day he decided he needed to get back to work, his wife 'rolled me out

Hmmm. Sometimes there are other things you weren't expecting like intruders who sit on your lap while writing and demand attention.

through the kitchen and down the newly installed wheelchair ramp into the back hall. She had made me a wonderful little nest there: laptop and printer … pens, reference materials. … "Is it all right?" she asked. "It's gorgeous," I said, and hugged her' (323-324).

This was a writer at the height of his fame reduced to a pop-up desk in the hallway. Yet, he didn't feel reduced. He just wanted to write.

STEP 3

DO THE ARITHMETIC

WE CAN'T AVOID IT; we need to do some sums.

Locate the number of words you wrote during each of the Spontaneous Writing exercises.

Add the two up - Exercise 1 + Exercise 2 = Total

Divide Total by 2

This now gives you an average of the number of words you write in 10 minutes.

Write   your   average   here   (or   elsewhere)
. . . .

I'm guessing that your average is somewhere between 150 - 450 words. That's quite a range because no two writers are exactly the same. If yours
lies outside of this range – that's no problem. It's
yours you'll be working with anyway.

"Just a darn minute! — Yesterday
you said that X equals **two!**"

Just to get us started, let's say you write an average
of 200 words in 10 minutes. If you only wrote for
10 minutes, but every day for 365 days (Yes,
Christmas Day too – get up before the children or
the pets. You'll need to get your writing self-satisfied
before all the rest of that begins!), that means:

200 x 365 = 73,000 words in a year. That's quite a
lot of words and is almost a novel. I'm talking about
the first draft, of course.

Let's say you estimate your writing project to be 100,000 words. So:

100,000 divided by 365 = 274 words in 10 minutes per day (first draft).

That's great! Easy! Provided you did work every day for just 10 minutes.

STEP 4

RESET THE TARGET

NOW GO BACK to **YOUR LONG-TERM GOAL** where you wrote down an estimation of the number of words and when you wanted to have this writing projected completed.

Let's say you did have the goal of 100,000 words of your first draft in one year.

Using the process above, you know that you need to write 274 useable words in 10 minutes, 365 days of the year.

However, you've calculated that you only write 180 words in 10 minutes. You have a couple of options. You are going to have to, either:

- extend your 10 minutes to 15 minutes, OR
- write more words in the available 10 minutes (i.e. write faster).

Let's say that your goal was to have 100,000 words of your first draft written in 6 months (183 days).

That's okay; we can work that out. So ...

100,000 words divided by 183 days = 547 words per day in ....

Hmmm. If you're writing an average of 180 or even 200 words in 10 minutes, then it's unlikely that you're going to write words of much quality by speeding up to 547. And you'll be exhausted. There's only one thing for it. If you really want to meet that deadline, then ...

You're going to have to increase the number of minutes you write per day.

If you increase to 30 minutes per day, every day for six months (183 days), then:

180 words per 10 minutes in 30 minutes = 540 words; 200 words per 10 minutes in 30 minutes = 600 words

600 words x 183 days = 109,800 words

BINGO!

If your original goal was to have the final draft completed in a year, then readjust accordingly, but remember not to compromise the quality of the work for the sake of a deadline.

Okay, you have your first draft done. Now you can use those 10 minutes a day to rework and refine. It's not possible for me to estimate how long this will take because it will depend on how much redrafting needs to be done, but some advice: Do it properly. Don't let the deadline, especially if self-imposed, determine the quality of the work.

If you know there will be non-writing periods (travel, hospitalisation etc.), then you'll need to renegotiate the timeline and number of words per day. Just use the same method as above.

THE POINT OF RESISTANCE

 YOU'VE PROBABLY ALREADY DISCOVERED that there's a point at which you no longer feel the words flowing, and your creativity feels as though it's drying up. Hopefully, that's not going to happen in as little as 10 minutes, but in those times when you do have a run at it – a few hours to spare - you find that you begin to burn out perhaps two hours in. Your resistance point is a personal one. Some writers will do marathons, others who feel burnt out after 500 words, but an average is around 1500 words in a single session. Generally, a professional writer will work towards 1500 words per day, every day.

If your target requires that you write a number of words per session that exceeds your point of resistance, you will need to establish some strategies for dealing with that. Of course, you can change the target date, but overcoming the resistance point can be achieved by breaking up the daily target into smaller sessions. Take a break. Stephen King, Charles Darwin, Albert Einstein and many other creative, gifted people have extolled the virtues of going for a walk – the 'daily constitutional'. When we take a break, the intense focus in the frontal cortex is relaxed, and neurons are free to fire in a broader range, accessing other information that feeds creative thought. If fitting around working life or other, try to find some other time in that day to continue. It might mean getting up earlier, or going to bed later, or deciding not to go to that party at the weekend …

Now you can rework the timetable. Perhaps by this point, you will have an idea that you can free up more time, but to help you along, I've included some ideas below.

HOW TO BECOME A TIME THIEF

IF YOU'VE BEEN FOLLOWING my advice, and my personal story, you might be thinking, 'surely she didn't do all that in just 10 minutes a day. It would take years!'

Good thinking. You're right.

A good deal of it - Master of Science, Master of Arts (first novel), PhD (second novel) while teaching full-time and having the rest of my life - began in that minimum of 10 minutes every day. And, yes, it did take years to do it all, but I reset the target to 20 minutes, and I also became a masterful time thief. I did reset the target when I had deadlines and adjusted my personal timetable accordingly. Some of the big and little thefts of time while I was working full time were:

- I used long service leave to 'act out' being a writer to see if I wanted that lifestyle. A daily routine of writing with the goal of 1,000-1500 words per day. (I also travelled, spent time with family and friends and did all the other things I love to do – reading, yoga, good times.)
- I used annual holidays to increase my 10-minute-per-day schedule, again leaving plenty of time to have a holiday!
- I probably shouldn't admit to this one, but I took a sickie (only one, I promise) to spend in the State Library to have an intensive writing day.
- I got up earlier on the weekend to write before the family did so that I could satisfy the writing self and then have time to devote to them. An interesting comment from one of my children was: 'Mum, when do you do it all?' I became and am still, to a certain degree, the invisible worker chipping away at my dreams.
- I don't drive and so use public transport regularly – ideal writing or revision time.
- **I became opportunistic**. This is an important one. Use the time that's floating. I always have a notebook or piece of paper and pen or include Notes in my phone when an idea strikes. This could be an extra 10 minutes in your day you weren't

expecting: a train delay, waiting for a program to load, a late guest speaker …. Once you've trained yourself to write without necessarily being in the mood (as a result of the 10-minute/spontaneous writing method), you'll get something of worth down quickly.

- If writing in the morning, reduce the number of things you need to do first thing. For example, lay out your clothes the night before, so you're not having to spend time in front of the wardrobe wondering or ironing.
- Make your lunch and/or children's lunches the night before.

Another tactic in my life of crime as a time thief is to be organised with other tasks (working life, home life) that need to be completed. These include:

- Tackling the largest jobs first. Though you might not feel like doing these straight up, once they're out of the way, you'll 'breeze' through the smaller tasks, and the target of completion will seem closer and more achievable. Not only can this method speed up the process of completion and thus provide you with more writing time, but it's also a bit of an insurance policy that the big ones will be done because, if left to

later, there are all sorts of things that can
go wrong: a family emergency, a bout of
the flu … Smaller tasks might still be done
in these circumstances.

A personal anecdote: I can locate the moment this
strategy became embedded in my psyche, and it all
had to do with segments of an orange. Bear with
me. I remember that I was very young and we were
at the beach. Our grandmother was peeling an orange and called my sister and me over. She had two
unevenly divided orange segments in her hand, and
she offered them to me first. I thought that I was
getting the whole orange (that she'd peel another for
my sister) and thought I'd choose the smaller section
first, then savour the larger. After I'd chosen the
smaller one (yes, you guessed it), granny passed the
larger one to my sister. I was devastated (I was
young, that's my excuse). I learned a very important
lesson in that moment, that if you leave the larger
portions until later, you might never get to them.

- Doing the sums. As a teacher then and
  now, I have many corrections to complete
  by a specific date. I'm the sort of person
  who can't really settle down to write if I
  have other commitments, so I like to clear
  the decks, but also in a professional
  manner. Using the method above, I set a
  target for completion, divide the number

of days I have given myself by the number of corrections to determine a daily number. However, I rarely do only the daily amount. Let's say I have 100 corrections to do in 10 days; that's 10 per day. If I do 12 on one day, I don't consider that I'll only do 8 the next; rather, I'll try to match it with 12 or at least the original 10. This way, I'll complete them before the original date set, giving myself more time to write!

- Rewarding. I love the sense of completing something and buying time as well for writing. As an incentive, I have a small reward waiting for when I've finished the task. It's usually something simple like - the latest yoga magazine. I'll buy it and leave it on the desk, and I don't open it until I'm finished the task. That way, it 'tastes sweeter' because I can truly relax and read at my leisure without any guilt.

'But Amanda,' you say, 'this is boring. I thought creative writing was supposed to be enjoyable, give me freedom, make me feel warm and fuzzy because it's a self-concordant goal. Now I just feel like I'm back in Mr Stricken's mathematics class!'

I understand. There's something else you might be thinking. 'Isn't it just a bit self-indulgent, stealing time to follow a dream (now a goal) when I might not be good anyway?'

Fair enough. But let me share the relevant part of a blog post I wrote a while ago just after my mother died - I hope it puts your mind at rest.

A NOBLE PROFESSION

In a recent creative writing class, I asked the students what value they thought a writer had in society. I think the question arose from my decision to leave the very noble profession of full-time teaching to follow my dream to be a writer. How self-indulgent! Had I lost my place in society? Was I no longer being of service? How could I compare my contribution with those who comfort the sick, the dying, the drug-affected, the battered .... We had a great conversation - my wonderful class and I - and I realised that, apart from the love and support of family and friends, it was reading that helped carry me through life's dark times. The death of a loved one takes you to dark places. When this happened to me, I scanned my bookshelf searching for relief. I by-passed tomes full of weighty words and deep philosophies and instead picked out one that I might normally 'hide' from serious literature-minded friends. Light and bright, food, love, good times and pretty shallow.

I thank that author for the comfort and the release from the heavy reality of my loss, for the half hours at a time where I was liberated and felt a return of joy. She may never know the effect of her 'self-indulgent' profession, but it's answered the question for me. Do writers have a valuable role in society? Absolutely.

FLOW OR IMMERSION

POSITIVE PSYCHOLOGY TELLS us that experiences of flow or immersion contribute to our sense of wellbeing. As writers, we know that, and you might well have recorded earlier that this is one of your reasons for writing.

However, like so many things that are good for us and make us feel better – exercise, yoga, meditation, practising a musical instrument, learning to cook – there can be a reluctance/resistance to

QUITE INTERESTING ¶

'People who set goals are more likely to succeed than people who don't and are more likely to experience hope, optimism and experiences of flow' (Csikszentmihayli 2002). ¶
¶

do it. I mentioned earlier that immersion was the one thing I resisted because I didn't want to have to come out of it!

It's a common experience that when we are left to our own devices (e.g. using a start-of-the-art home gymnasium; rolling out the yoga mat on the bedroom floor; sitting down to the piano; sitting still and allowing our thoughts to calm), no matter how good the feeling during and at the end, it just seems to be harder to do it than say – going to the gym, attending a yoga class or meditation retreat or hiring a music teacher.

For some, perhaps many writers, it's the same story. No matter how comfortable the desk and study, it's hard to get going. For this reason, writing classes are a popular choice. Like the gym instructor, music or yoga teacher, or Zen master, a good writing instructor can help to motivate a writer, improve existing skills and foster the development of new ones. However, once the class or course is over, you're on your own and quite likely back where you started.

You need strategies; you need to self-instruct. The minimum 10-minute ritual above is designed to help you to take charge of your writing life. How you spend the 10 minutes is in your hands. If practised regularly, being able to immerse yourself, to enter into the flow of the writing process should take less time and thus the quality, and perhaps the quantity, of words should improve.

So far, I've suggested the following to help you slide into the writing process with ease:

- Keep writing, no matter what mumbo-jumbo you come up with and allow the writing itself to generate momentum.
- Borrow lines from your favourite author to get you going. If the writing is useable for your writing task, just make sure you get rid of those lead-ins.

Here's another one:

- Leave the last sentence for the day unfinished. It's easier to ride an existing idea to the end of the sentence and beyond than to start 'cold' the next day.

OTHER IDEAS TO
ASSIST FLOW

THERE ARE other things you can do. Yoga has been an important part of my life for over forty years. While I do not intend to 'push' this on you because I appreciate that it's not for everyone, I'll at least offer some of the reasons why it could assist you to immerse into your writing more quickly. Of course, there might be other things that you know work for you, like listening to your favourite or inspiring music while you write, but the following are the benefits of yoga, in my experience. [When I use the word 'yoga' here, I'm not just talking about 'asana' or the exercises that are commonly mistaken for being yoga. They're just a component of a larger picture that includes - breath control (pranayama) and the ultimate purpose of yoga according to the Patanjali – meditation.] Yoga can help to:

- Focus awareness or attention
- Calm the mind and body
- Increase creativity
- Reinforce self-concordant goals
- Assist the development of resilience

These are big claims, and I don't have the research evidence to support them; it is merely my experience from almost a lifetime of yoga, and I'm no adept.

Yoga's ultimate goal – meditation - has a powerful relationship with another gem of positive psychology: mindfulness.

If it sounds too fluffy for you, that's okay; skip the next bit and go to Resilience. You might need it.

MINDFULNESS

Mindfulness requires that we bring our complete attention to the experience of the present moment.

By observing the state of your mind – its fluctuations and 'monkey chatter' - you train yourself to become more focused.

When we do something that we love, like writing or reading, going for a run, yoga, solving a complex math problem, the 'monkey mind' calms (the limbic system is subdued).

I remember sitting in the back of our family car, reading as my parents said their final farewells to the host of another Sunday event. Said host was tapping on the window of the car to attract my attention. I was so totally absorbed in reading (probably the next-in-the-series Famous Five adventure) I didn't hear him (and was duly scolded by my mother for my rudeness!). The same thing happens now in the coffee shops where I tend to do a lot of my writing. People wonder how I can write with so much noise, but I have trained myself – through the 10-minute intensives each morning, and no doubt yoga has had a great effect too. The immersion is rapid, focused and everything else, but my cup of coffee next to me disappears.

I'm certain you know this feeling well. It's not unique to me, or yogis for that matter. 'Time disappears' is the frequent comment.

This is flow and is enhanced by becoming mindful – in the now. Being in the moment of writing might well have been one of your responses.

If it's difficult for you to enter into that space, I'm suggesting that yoga and meditation, among other methods, can assist you.

RESILIENCE
WHEN THE PLAN GOES AWRY

DEAR WRITER

I know that no matter how carefully we might plan things, something just might come in and shake the tree. I mentioned earlier that we became the carers of two of our grandchildren, who were just five and six years old. Aside from the emotional response, all round, my writing life certainly was under strain. I had to abandon my morning trip to the coffee shop, but not my morning writing. Once they were safely tucked into school and childminding, I used the train journey to work to write – at this stage, I was still working full time and midway through my PhD (which included the second novel). As the children got older, I would resume my routine at the coffee shop. I claimed it back, and I gave myself permission to do so. The children understood that this was my time and that they would have the rest of my waking hours.

My first novel was about to be published when my daughter came down with a life-threatening illness, and my partner and I found ourselves caring for a third grandchild (her daughter) while she recovered.

On the day the novel was published, my daughter was scheduled for heart surgery, but it was postponed. While she slept, I caught the tram to my favourite book shop on the other side of the city. '*My book's being published today*,' I told the manager, feeling all the while that I was in some kind of dream. He was very excited for me, disappeared and came back with a few copies that he placed on the New Releases shelf. I took a photo (all still too surreal for many reasons), crossed to a well-known and loved Melbourne coffee shop and ordered a treat to celebrate on my own. I caught the tram to a different hospital to see my mother who was about to undergo exploratory surgery, then back to my daughter, then to my partner, who was recovering from his second knee replacement, picked up the children and home. Somewhere in all of that, I found time to write. In the chaos surrounding me, it was like a precious gem that centred me because it had become a significant part of who I am.

In its simplest form, resilience is the capacity to recover quickly from difficulties. There is no doubt about it – some people find it easier to recover more quickly than others, and I don't want to suggest here that it is something that can be easily remedied. Like our self-esteem, resilience, or lack of, is a result of our experiences and so very personal to us. However, I'd like to offer that if you work through the above process of goal setting and stick to it, you will help to increase your sense of resilience, if only by a little.

Ben-Shahar believes that goals communicate to ourselves and to others that we are capable of overcoming obstacles. 'I believe that goals are indispensable to a happy life' (65).

I've offered, too, that yoga/meditation can help - to centre ourselves, to see ourselves as perfectly imperfect and that the trials and tribulations that occur to all of us at some point are transient and can only 'touch' us as much as we allow. It can help, too, to look back at those times in your life when you have bounced back and build confidence in that ability. Now that's worth remembering, so write it here:

....

....

....

If writing is important to you, and I think if you've come this far, it is, then resolve that you will stick to it – take the journey, bumps and all. It's a great one.

I include below the blog post that I wrote the day I handed in my PhD thesis:

Between the Lines

I handed in my thesis today for examination. It's taken me nine years. As I checked it over before submission, I thought how pristine it all looked. In fact, it looked as though I really knew what I was doing and, really ... why had it taken nine years! What will the Examiner's think? I'll find out in a few months, and no doubt it will rebound with, I hope, not too many bits and pieces to tidy up. What they won't see, though, is the life between the lines. As I readied the manuscript, I thought about all that has happened in nine years. I've already alluded to some of those things in previous posts, and I don't want to appear as though I think I'm the only one who has the lion's share of life's dramas and highs. Quite the opposite. Reflecting on what had been happening in the foreground of my life while the

thesis sulked in the background just makes me re-
alise how very frail and beautiful it is to be human.
For my own record, I'm recording some of those
things here, just to remind myself that I have
achieved a personal monumental milestone. Here's
what lies between the lines of my spotless manuscript: births of five grandchildren; full-time care
of two of them; death of my beloved father; the
publication of my first novel; the death-defying feat
of my daughter; my partner's painful recovery, the
jump from the mothership of full-time employ-
ment; good times with my mother; my beautiful
mother's death; good times with family; good times
with good friends; love; food; simple and greater
pleasures; the joy of teaching creative writing and
yoga; the gift of brilliant supervisors; the excitement
of starting a third novel; the recognition of the pre-
ciousness of the extended family and any who come
under that umbrella; my home; my pond; my cat;
my books; my children; my partner. How blessed I
am. No, the Examiners won't see what lies between
the lines.

I know that no matter how much you might plan,
life can have other ideas. Though we like to think it,
not everything is in our control. However, there are
still things you can control – how you respond, how
you adapt.

In *On Writing: A Memoir of the Craft*, Stephen King
tells of how he always dreamed of having a massive

oak slab for a desk that would dominate his spacious, skylighted study. He got it, but years later, he swapped it for a smaller, handmade one that he put in a corner under the eave.

'It starts with this: put your desk in the corner, and every time you sit down there to write, remind yourself why it isn't in the middle of the room. Life isn't a support-system for art. It's the other way around' (112).

It's not just the really tough times that require our resilience. The simple fact is the 'downside' of our writing lives will/might include:

- Periods of self-doubt that plague us
- Inspiration and creativity that eludes us
- Rejections from publishers that flatten us

- Negative comments from others that can drain us
- Niggling health issues that tax us
- Isolation that confines us

And then there's the big one:

- It can be hard work and for little gain

Is that right? 'For little gain'?

Let's revisit a couple of those responses you wrote earlier:

What were the reasons you came to writing?

Why do you like to write? What do you get out of it?

Your reasons are worthy. The writing is worthy. You are worthy. Keep reminding yourself of this and remember that those who establish and work towards self-concordant goals are happier than those who don't.

When talking of goals, my yoga teacher uses the analogy of the archer. If the target shifts, but the stance is strong, the focus directed and the aim true, the archer is poised to follow.

You might have to reconsider the timeline, but don't give up on the goal.

Good luck.

Amanda

Dear reader,

We hope you enjoyed reading *Time Management for Writers*. Please take a moment to leave a review, even if it's a short one. Your opinion is important to us.

Discover more books by Amanda Apthorpe at https://www.nextchapter.pub/authors/amanda-apthorpe

Want to know when one of our books is free or discounted? Join the newsletter at http://eepurl.com/bqqB3H

Best regards,

Amanda Apthorpe and the Next Chapter Team

You might also like:
Finding Your Writer's Voice by Amanda Apthorpe

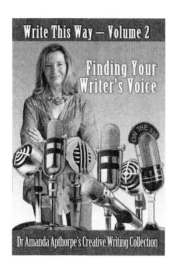

To read the first chapter for free, please head to:
https://www.nextchapter.pub/books/finding-your-
writer's-voice

REFERENCES

Amabile, T. (1985). 'Motivation and creativity: effects of motivational orientation on creative writers', in *Journal of Personality and Social Psychology*, 1985, Vol. 48, No. 2, 393-399

Apthorpe, A. (2014) 'Minding the Gap between Aspiration and Achievement', in *Minding The Gap: Writing Across Thresholds and Fault Lines*. The Referred Proceedings of The 19th Conference of the Australasian Association of Writing Programs, 2014, Wellington NZ

Baer, J. and McKool, S. (2009) 'How Rewards and Evaluations Can Undermind Creativity (and How to Prevent This)', in *The Psychology of Creative Writing* ed. Kaufman, S.B. and Kaufman, J. C (eds) Cambridge University Press, New York.

Bane, R. (2010). 'The Writers Brain: What Neurology Tells Us about Teaching Creative Writing', in *Creative Writing: Teaching Theory & Practice 41*, Vol. 2. No. 1. 41-50

Ben-Shahar, T. (2007). 'Setting Goals', in *Happier*, McGraw Hill, USA

Czikszentmihayli, M. (2002). *Flow: The Classic Work on How to Achieve Happiness*, Rider, London

Faucheux, L. (2012). 'Aligning Strengths with Goals: Creating a Self-Concordant Journey', 03/01/2012, https://www.ncda.org

Locke, E. A., Latham, G.P. (Eds). (2013). *New developments in goal setting and task performance*, Routledge, New York

Lyubomirsky, S. (2010). 'Committing to your goals', in *The How of Happiness*, Piatkus, London

King, S. (2000). *On Writing, A Memoir of the Craft*, Hodder & Stoughton, London

Sternberg, R.J. (2006). 'The Nature of Creativity', in *Creativity Research Journal*, 2006, Vol. 18, No. 1, 87-98

Watson, S.J. (2013). 'What a Creative Writing Course taught me', in *The Guardian*, 18 January 2013

Zapetakis, L.A, Bouranta, N. & Moustakis, V. (2010). 'On the relationship between individual creativity and time management', in *Thinking Skills and Creativity*, Vol. 5, No. 1, 23-32

ACKNOWLEDGMENTS

This series is such a pleasure to write and is made even more so by the generosity of others. Thanks go to my partner, Chris, for his wonderful support; to Roscoe Maddalon for his encouragement and suggestions; to my first publisher Helen Goltz and Atlas Productions, whose enthusiasm, expertise and belief in me has been this author's great fortune; and to Next Chapter for the opportunity to re-publish this work and for the care the team take in its production.

APPENDIX
JOURNAL ENTRIES

DAY	
1	LENGTH OF TIME WRITING: REFLECTION:
2	LENGTH OF TIME WRITING: REFLECTION:
3	LENGTH OF TIME WRITING: REFLECTION:
4	LENGTH OF TIME WRITING: REFLECTION:
5	LENGTH OF TIME WRITING: REFLECTION:

| 6 | LENGTH OF TIME WRITING: |
| | REFLECTION: |

| 7 | LENGTH OF TIME WRITING: |
| | REFLECTION: |

| 8 | LENGTH OF TIME WRITING: |
| | REFLECTION: |

| 9 | LENGTH OF TIME WRITING: |
| | REFLECTION: |

| 10 | LENGTH OF TIME WRITING: |
| | REFLECTION: |

11	LENGTH OF TIME WRITING: REFLECTION:
12	LENGTH OF TIME WRITING: REFLECTION:
13	LENGTH OF TIME WRITING: REFLECTION:
14	LENGTH OF TIME WRITING: REFLECTION:

ABOUT THE AUTHOR

Amanda Apthorpe is a published writer of fiction, non-fiction, and is an educator. Effective time management skills are a signature strength, evident in the completion of a Master of Science, a Master of Arts, a Philosophy Doctorate and two novels while working as a full-time science teacher and raising a family.

In 2011, after the publication of her first novel, *Whispers in the Wiring*, and after twenty-five years teaching science, Amanda took a new path to follow her dream as a writer and teacher; to 'walk the home strait' with her widowed mother and, with her partner Chris, raise two grandchildren who had been placed in their care. During this time, she completed a certificate of training to enable her to teach creative writing in the TAFE sector, trained to be a yoga instructor, and completed her PhD, which culminated in the publication of her second novel, *A Single Breath*.

Amanda has presented papers on creative writing and time management at conferences in Wellington

NZ and London UK, has been interviewed on radio, and has convened workshops on time management for Writers Victoria. She teaches at Swinburne University of Technology, Victoria University, and the Centre for Adult Education.

In addition to the *Write This Way* series, Amanda has four novels: *Whispers in the Wiring*, *A Single Breath*, *Hibernia*, and *One Core Belief* published by Next Chapter.

Time Management For Writers
ISBN: 978-4-86752-543-2
Large Print

Published by
Next Chapter
1-60-20 Minami-Otsuka
170-0005 Toshima-Ku, Tokyo
+818035793528

18th August 2021

9 784867 525432